# *The New Tiffany Table Settings*

# THE NEW TIFFANY TABLE SETTINGS

*By John Loring and Henry B. Platt*

*Doubleday & Company, Inc., Garden City, New York*

DESIGNED BY LAURENCE ALEXANDER

Library of Congress Cataloging in Publication Data

Tiffany and Company, New York.
The new Tiffany table settings.

1. Table setting and decoration.   I. Loring, John.
II Platt, Henry B.   III. Title.
TX879.T48     1981     642:7
ISBN: 0-385-15849-1 (hc)
ISBN: 0-385-23758-8 (pbk.)
Library of Congress Catalog Card Number 80-919
Copyright © 1981 by Tiffany & Co., Inc.

# *Foreword*

The history of modern table setting opened on a momentous day in 1633 when Charles I of England declared once and for all that "it is decent to use a fork." Since then the table's arts have prospered while all manner of refinements and curiosities have been seen, some practical, some stylish, some simply preposterous.

Tables are as much as ever stages that we set for action, miniature theaters of social behavior where a good percentage of every life is played out.

There love blossoms or withers, careers are made or undone, fortunes are founded or squandered. The table is a place for enjoyment, for wit, for discovery, for celebration, for art, for intrigue. There we set out props that forecast the order of events and that imply whatever we desire from social exchange.

Anyone can set a table, and anyone can set it well with whatever means are available, provided that imagination and vitality are both brought to the task. The success of a table setting depends not on financial considerations but on having a point of view, on having a personal style rather than timidly depending on bland and faceless conventionalities.

In the pages that follow, there are table settings done at the request of Tiffany & Co. by some seventy-five well-known personalities of society, entertainment, the arts, business, and design. They have brought to their settings the same flair and authority that have brought them such remarkable success in the world. Each setting is in a way the self-portrait of its author.

There are no answers given to the question of how to set a table, but the collective answer is: "Do what you want, and do your best."

In 1808 the great French authority on entertaining Alexandre Balthasar Laurent Grimod de La Reynière published his famed *Manuel des Amphitryons.* In it he exhorted the good host or hostess not to hold back or to be ashamed of originality and generosity, and his advice remains valid: "Don't be afraid to put your fortune in evidence and do honor to it; do nothing to pardon its sources as there is no more honorable way to use it than to offer food."

# Contents

Foreword/V

# THE DINNER

The Tiffany Dinner/*Henry B. Platt*/2

Dîner pour le Premier Ministre/*La Vicomtesse Jacqueline de Ribes*/8

Before the Theater/*Mrs. Vincent Astor*/12

Le Dîner en Ville/*Prince and Princess Edouard de Lobkowicz*/16

Manhattan/*Mrs. Walter Hoving*/18

Dîner Parisien/*Mrs. Antenor Patino*/22

Penthouse Party/*Eugenia Sheppard and Earl Blackwell*/26

Dinner Before the Opera/*Mrs. Gordon Getty*/28

Midnight in the Wine Cellar/*Mrs. Oscar S. Wyatt, Jr.*/32

Opus 23/*Juan Montoya*/36

A Small Candlelight Supper/*Mrs. Christian de Guigne*/38

Le Dîner en Rose/*Mrs. Guilford Dudley*/42

Dinner Before the Theater/*Mrs. Edward Byron Smith*/46

Centennial Anniversary Celebration/*Mrs. James Hoban Harris*/50

# ALL FOR ONE

Breakfast in Bed/*Mario Buatta*/54

Tropical Morning/*Tiffany & Co.*/56

TV Dinner/*Mrs. Thomas L. Kempner*/58

Dinner with Voltaire/*Diana Vreeland*/60

Dinner in Jail/*Andy Warhol*/62

# TÊTE-À-TÊTE

Dinner for Two/*Cary Grant*/68

Garden Party/*Gloria Vanderbilt*/72

Monday Night Football/*Mrs. Alfred Bloomingdale*/74

Dinner and a Show/*Mark Hampton*/76

Two for Lunch: Still Two for Dinner/*Elsa Peretti*/78

Regency Safari/*Lee Radziwill*/82

A Romantic Repast/*Mrs. William Sarnoff*/84

Soirée Intime/*Mrs. Aileen Mehle (Suzy Knickerbocker)*/86

Tête-à-Tête/*MAC II*/88

The Night Before Breakfast at Tiffany's/*Dexter Design, Inc.*/90

Gypsy Tearoom à la Tiffany/*McMillen, Inc.*/92

Matinee Day Lunch/*Lionel Larner for Mia Farrow*/94

Lunch for Two Writers on Long Island/*Rosamond Bernier Russell*/98

A Thousand and One Nights/*The Honorable Joanne King Herring*/100

Supper After Scheherazade/*Mrs. Lawrence Copley Thaw*/102

Christmas Eve/*Tiffany & Co.*/104

New Year's Eve/*Tiffany & Co.*/106

# MORNING

Breakfast with Houseguests/*Mr. and Mrs. James Stewart*/110

Breakfast in Cuernavaca/*Tiffany & Co.*/112

Primavera/*John Saladino*/114

A Family Country Breakfast/*Mrs. John R. Drexel III*/116

A Connecticut Hunt Breakfast/*Mrs. William F. Buckley, Jr.*/118

Christmas Morning/*Tiffany & Co.*/122

# NOON

Lunch for Two/*Mrs. Henry Kissinger*/126

A Small In-office Lunch/*John T. Sargent*/128

A Client Lunch at Wells, Rich, Greene, Inc./*Mrs. Harding Lawrence*/130

A Thai Terrace Lunch/*Mr. and Mrs. Tony Duquette*/132

Déjeuner Normand/*Prince and Princess Edouard de Lobkowicz*/134

For Julia Child and Company/*Julia Child*/136

Connecticut Sunday Lunch/*Angela Cummings*/138

Country Buffet at Templeton/*C. Z. Guest*/142

Lunch in a Loft/*John Loring*/144

Lunch in the Corporate Boardroom/*Letitia Baldrige*/148

First Birthday/*Lorna de Wangen*/150

# NIGHT

Dinner with Your Best Friend/*Françoise de la Renta*/154

Triangle/*Ruben de Saavedra*/156

A Timeless Table/*Van Day Truex*/158

Supper with Arthur Smith/*Arthur Smith*/160

Dîner: Rouge et Noir/*Lily Auchincloss*/162

Food for Thought/*Robert Currie and Christine Maly*/166

Dinner for Four/*Angelo Donghia*/168

Dinner/*Douglas Fairbanks, Jr.*/170

Country Supper on the Back Porch/*Mrs. Angier Biddle Duke*/172

Heart to Heart/*Mrs. Donald Newhouse*/174

Exposure/*Mrs. John Murchison*/176

Formally Informal Wine Cellar Supper/*Mrs. James D. Robinson, Jr.*/178

At Home on the Avenue/*Mrs. Seymour Berkson*/180

# TEA AND COFFEE

Fin d'Été/*Paloma Picasso*/184

Le Café au Salon Rouge/*Mme Émile Aillaud*/188

Tea on the Porch/*Suzanne and Carleton Varney*/192

Tea for More Than Two/*Mrs. John Pierrepont*/194

Victoriana/*Robert Denning and Vincent Fourcade*/198

Sunday Tea/*Mrs. Denton A. Cooley*/200

The Fledermaus Café/*after Josef Hoffmann: Tiffany & Co.*/202

Dessert Party After the Winter Antiques Show Opening/
*Mrs. Cruger D. G. Fowler*/204

# THE GREAT OUTDOORS

The Golfer's Lunch/*Bob Hope*/210

"Roughing It" with a Picnic/*Mrs. Alfred Kennedy*/214

Eternal Triangle/*Gene Moore*/216

Veranda Picnic/*Mrs. Henry Parish II*/218

The Mysterious, Romantic Picnic on the Shores of Lake Michigan/
*Suzanne Clarke Falk*/220

Dinner at the Beach/*Tiffany & Co.*/222

Hunting Picnic/*Diana Rigg*/224

*Photography Credits*/228
*Acknowledgments*/229

# THE DINNER

---

The Tiffany Dinner / Henry B. Platt

Dîner pour le Premier Ministre / La Vicomtesse Jacqueline de Ribes

Before the Theater / Mrs. Vincent Astor

Le Dîner en Ville / Prince and Princess Edouard de Lobkowicz

Manhattan / Mrs. Walter Hoving

Dîner Parisien / Mrs. Antenor Patino

Penthouse Party / Eugenia Sheppard and Earl Blackwell

Dinner Before the Opera / Mrs. Gordon Getty

Midnight in the Wine Cellar / Mrs. Oscar S. Wyatt, Jr.

Opus 23 / Juan Montoya

A Small Candlelight Supper / Mrs. Christian de Guigne

Le Dîner en Rose / Mrs. Guilford Dudley

Dinner Before the Theater / Mrs. Edward Byron Smith

Centennial Anniversary Celebration / Mrs. James Hoban Harris

---

# THE TIFFANY DINNER
## *Henry B. Platt*

No other American artist/designer had such a varied, long, and brilliant career as Louis Comfort Tiffany. His name is synonymous with Tiffany glass and its incomparable iridescent surfaces; however, Tiffany was not only a "rebel" genius of the glass industry; he was for over sixty active years an accomplished painter and designer of ceramics, enamels, jewels, fabrics, bronzes, lamps, and complete interiors. He was also an accomplished party giver, bon vivant, and arbiter of taste.

The grandeur and brilliance of Tiffany's fêtes and masques were legendary in New York. Cholly Knickerbocker summed it up in the New York *American* following "L.C.T.'s" birthday breakfast and masque, "The Quest of Beauty," given on February 19, 1916: "We all felt like acclaiming him the most wonderful of guides in leading us to Beauty, and being so successful in the quest."

When only thirty, Tiffany founded Louis C. Tiffany & Co. Associated Artists, and two years later, in 1880, received the commission for what remains one of New York's greatest interiors, the Veterans' Room of the Knickerbocker Greys' Seventh Regiment Armory. With its massive chain-wrapped columns, its opalescent blue Tiffany glass-tile fireplace, and its elaborate bands of scrolling Celtic interlace that embellish everything from the ponderous ax-hewn soffit beams to the intricately carved oak wainscoting, this early Art Nouveau masterpiece is bold without ostentation and typifies the great originality and virility that Tiffany brought to the world of decoration.

Here on the one hundredth anniversary of the Veterans' Room's creation, L.C.T.'s great-grandson, Henry B. Platt, vice-chairman of Tiffany & Co., has re-created a table setting in the style of his great-grandfather.

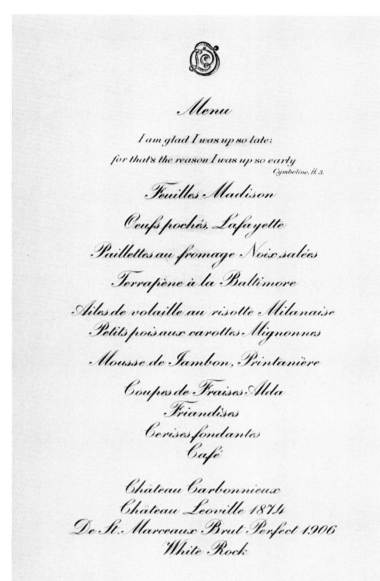

The iridescent "Favrile" Tiffany glass service of stemware, carafes, salts, finger bowls, ice plates, and compotes was a wedding present to Mr. Platt's mother from her grandfather, Louis Comfort Tiffany. Flat silver is "Olympian," created by Tiffany & Co. in 1878 and still made from the original steel dies. Underplates are Spode's "Sheffield" in the simple gold and white favored by Tiffany, and the table linen, in traditional late-nineteenth-century style, is heavy Irish damask overlaid with an antique Venetian lace runner set. Four magnificent bronze and Favrile glass ball Tiffany Studios candlesticks illuminate this scene, in which Louis Comfort Tiffany would have felt totally at home.

# DÎNER POUR LE PREMIER MINISTRE
## *La Vicomtesse Jacqueline de Ribes*

Marcel Proust's *fin-de-siècle* France had a fondness for decking its traditions of lordly hospitality in the fronds and flowers of the conservatory. Its interior decorations recalled in part the royal palace and in part the Jardin des Plantes.

The Proustian atmosphere survives in a few great Paris houses but nowhere more intact than at la Vicomtesse de Ribes's: "a privileged place" (to borrow a phrase from Proust) "in which one could pass only from surprise to delight."

The de Ribes *jardin d'hiver*, decorated for a dinner honoring the French Premier, recalls nothing so much as the Duc and Duchesse de Guermantes' fête for the Princesse de Parme in *The Remembrance of Things Past*.

The triumphant floral centerpieces are all of la Vicomtesse de Ribes's design. The table is set with a service of late-eighteenth-century Sèvres porcelain. The de Ribes family silver is after a Meissonier design, and the heavy cut-crystal water goblets, wineglasses, and champagne flutes are Tiffany's "Harcourt" by Baccarat and sit directly above the plates in the French manner.

The glass-roofed winter garden was decorated in the nineteenth century with *faux* marble columns framing eighteenth-century Beauvais hunting tapestries.

Marble busts of Roman emperors look on.

11

# BEFORE THE THEATER

*Mrs. Vincent Astor*

The days of Mrs. William Waldorf Astor, decked in diamond tiara and diamond stomacher, royally presiding over the Four Hundred at her Fifth Avenue and Sixty-fifth Street mansion have long faded into American social mythology. The more modest New York dinners of her granddaughter-in-law Mrs. Vincent Astor continue, however, to be as impeccably Astorian as followers of our great American dynasties could wish.

For an intimate pre–Broadway theater dinner, Mrs. Astor has chosen a richly gilt and painted "Flora Danica" porcelain dessert service, and "Olympian" vermeil, already a popular Tiffany pattern by 1895 when Mrs. William Astor built her Fifth Avenue mansion. There are antique finger bowls that belonged to Mrs. William Astor, and a set of "Koskull" etched crystal stemware copied from models made in 1790 for Baron Anders Koskull, founder of Sweden's Kosta glassworks. These remarkable glasses, although they relate to Louis XVI style, are closely akin to George III English crystal and not unlike glass used in America at the time John Jacob Astor arrived from Walldorf in 1783.

To break the essential regularity of formal settings, Mrs. Astor favors multiple bouquets in miniature vases. Here she uses a dozen or so small crystal pears and apples holding roses and freesias irregularly grouped about a crystal "sweetmeat tree," its hanging baskets brimming with flowers and crowned with strawberries.

Following the guests' departure for the theater, the dining room's set of four French Regency caned armchairs has been pushed back from the round Louis XVI table. An eighteenth-century French pastoral panel attributed to Jean Pillement backs the candlelit scene.

# LE DÎNER EN VILLE
## *Prince and Princess Edouard de Lobkowicz*

The Parisian dinner party is an event founded on ritual and tradition, built of the great cuisine and wines of France, and ornamented by spirited and witty conversation.

Here in the restrained and elegant home of the Prince and Princess Lobkowicz the table is formally set for sixteen. Early-nineteenth-century silver service plates by Odiot bear the Prince's arms. The flat silver combines the Lobkowicz arms with the royal French fleur-de-lis of the Princess (née Françoise de Bourbon-Parme).

There are four paneled "Harcourt" cut-crystal goblets at each place, and a charming collection of Tiffany's Spadini harlequin figurines sit about the "Chinese Bouquet" porcelain centerpiece.

Menus are engraved with the Prince's coronet and held by silver coins dating from the eighteenth century, when the Lobkowicz family held the right to coin money in the Austrian Empire.

Son Excellence
l'Ambassadeur d'Autriche

# MANHATTAN
## *Mrs. Walter Hoving*

---

The glittering glass and steel curtain-walled skyscrapers of Manhattan with their reflective skins and crisp-lined gravity-defying profiles inspired a setting by New York and Newport hostess Mrs. Walter Hoving (wife of Tiffany's long-time Chairman). Her "Manhattan" is at once traditional and innovative and filled with visual excitement.

In the midst of her tablescape, Mrs. Hoving builds a sparkling crystal city of massed pyramids, cones, prisms, and obelisks liberally and brightly lit by candles of varying heights, and sloping down at each end to miniature plantings of mixed white flowers. The highly polished table stays bare to mirror the scene. There are no porcelains, no patterns, and no colors to complicate this already abundant ensemble composed of only two elements, silver and glass.

A giant, wittily surrealistic pink-red flower, "Flying Rose," by Jane Pickens Hoving hovers above her idealized city's skyline, adding its strong visual drama and giving the generous glamour of this formal dinner setting a sense of warmhearted gaiety and humor.

Mrs. Hoving's English Regency dining room chairs are upholstered with tapestry seats specially designed for her by Jacques Muiden. Their assorted vegetable motifs coordinate with the whorls and garlands of a Portuguese floral tapestry carpet.

The reflections and facets of Mrs. Hoving's dinner setting are picked up and multiplied by paneled crystal dinner plates on sterling silver service plates, panel-cut "Elegance" goblets and champagne flutes, and intricately sculpted "Chrysanthemum" flat silver.

21

# DÎNER PARISIEN
## *Mrs. Antenor Patino*

Evenings promise nothing but pleasure at the legendary Patino entertainments. In the dining room, where every detail is a masterpiece of the decorative arts, the table is invariably laden with objects of great virtue. The food will be memorable. There will be guitarists in the background contributing to the general air of gaiety and celebration, while the carefully composed guest list will guarantee conversation as brilliant as the setting.

Here Mme Patino builds her table around an extraordinary Louis XV silver centerpiece made for the French royal family by François Thomas Germain in the mid-eighteenth century. Its overt grandeur is lightened by a tablecloth amusingly embroidered with musical motifs.

Place settings include seventeenth-century English silver service plates and contemporary "Nancy" cut-crystal stemware. The flat silver is a mixture of antique pieces with Tiffany's "Hamilton."

On the mantelpiece a bust of Mme de Wailly by the eighteenth-century sculptor Pageot is flanked by Johann Kändler Meissen swans mounted as candlesticks. The remarkable Louis XV clock above Mme de Wailly is by Jacques Caffiéri.

# PENTHOUSE PARTY
## *Eugenia Sheppard and Earl Blackwell*

Eugenia Sheppard, Queen of syndicated fashion columnists, and Earl Blackwell, King and President of the Celebrity Service and *Register,* take a break from work on their popular novels, which include *Crystal Clear* and *Skyrocket,* to entertain at an after-theater supper party in Mr. Blackwell's frescoed Manhattan ballroom.

"Framboise Rose" Private Stock china sits on a pale pink cloth along with "Hadeland" cut clear crystal and "Faneuil" flat silver.

Trompe l'oeil frescoes by W. J. Hankinson create a Mediterranean palazzo atmosphere.

There are ballroom chairs. A piano provides for the evening's spontaneous musical entertainments.

# DINNER BEFORE THE OPERA
## *Mrs. Gordon Getty*

The profligate attention to detail, the dizzying intricacy of textures and patterns, the heady but balanced richness of color, all contribute to the quiet excitement of this extraordinary setting that delights in its own opulence.

The tone is late-eighteenth-century, that happy period in history when luxury was contagious and the decorative arts were in flower.

The quality of every detail here in the Gordon Gettys' Pacific Heights dining room from the antique Ushak carpet to the candlelit Russian crystal chandelier is remarkable.

The table, surrounded by eighteenth-century Italian shield-back chairs, is covered in eighteenth-century French brocade. The Chinoiserie of the room's wall decorations is picked up in the setting by "Cirque Chinois" Tiffany Private Stock porcelain plates, the oriental motifs of "Audubon" vermeil flatware, vermeil pagodas, and ormolu mounted Ch'ien Lung polychromed porcelain figures of Chinamen holding censers. The engraved and gilded glasses are eighteenth-century Venetian. Flowers and candles are kept low, maintaining the pleasing density of the table's visual delights.

A silver coffee service with "Yellow Fish Scale" cups and "Feather Edge" silver spoons waits on the lacquered top of a richly carved and gilded eighteenth-century Portuguese table, in dramatic contrast to the Golden Gate Bridge seen beyond, across the Bay.

# MIDNIGHT IN THE WINE CELLAR

## Mrs. Oscar S. Wyatt, Jr.

Regiments of French Bordeaux and Burgundy bottles wearing their deep red caps watch over the wine cellar table. In this intimate setting the Oscar Wyatts leave behind the formality of their Houston house to entertain small groups of friends.

The air of old-world charm and the good life is pointed up by the familiar "Blue Onion" pattern of the china with its coordinated napkins, the sturdy "Metternich" crystal, and the handsome "King William" flat silver. A brightly direct red, white, and blue color scheme enlivens the atmosphere.

Although the Wyatts' wine cellar is above ground, Lynn Wyatt amuses herself by ornamenting the table with mushrooms, both crystal for decorative accents and real for place card holders.

Guests are provided with ample fur throws and shawls to ward off the simulated subterranean chill.

# OPUS 23

*Juan Montoya*

White orchids and cool fluorescent lighting, "Victoria" wineglasses on an industrial wire-glass tabletop, black Formica, pink cotton and satin napkins, Viennese café chairs, and Tiffany's "Hampton" flat silver, along with a dazzling array of contemporary Tiffany sterling silver, mix company on this table abandoned to the highly polished and structured luxury of 1980s New York.

The detached elegance, sophisticated surfaces, and ironclad composure of industrial materials could not be better domesticated than here by designer and high priest of "High Tech" Juan Montoya.

# A SMALL CANDLELIGHT SUPPER

## *Mrs. Christian de Guigne*

---

San Francisco is the most European of American cities. The spacious, expansive opulence of its great houses has more kinship with the villas of Cap Ferrat than with the industrialists' mansions of New York, yet it has an accent on comfort that is all-American.

In the well-balanced luxury of her San Francisco dining room, Mrs. Christian de Guigne sets a table for four. A linen and wool floral brocade in muted pastel tones, woven specially in Florence by Scalamandrè for Mrs. de Guigne, upholsters the room's comfortably "overstuffed" furniture and is used as a table cover as well. The upholstered armchairs at the table suggest that the evening's accent will be on good conversation, while the four "Paris" glasses at each place announce a properly complex and formal menu. "Shell and Thread" vermeil is turned down for an additional European note. A four-branch vermeil candelabrum draped in ivy lights and centers the table. Big bouquets of garden flowers sit about the room but not on the table itself, which is already amply in bloom with its "Scattered Flowers" Meissen porcelain set against the de Guigne floral brocade.

Pre-dinner drinks are served by the pool from simple silver beakers and a "Tiffany Swag" pitcher.

# LE DÎNER EN ROSE
## *Mrs. Guilford Dudley*

Floral table etiquette no longer dictates central hedgerows of palms and smilax, with asparagus ferns draped everywhere. Our contemporary settings at times banish flowers entirely and at others effectively include all and any of them, from artichokes to cymbidiums.

Palm Beach and Nashville hostess Jane Dudley (the wife of former Ambassador to Denmark Guilford Dudley) rightly feels that formal dinners are no time to hold back. She sets an intimate table for four around a forest of flowers whose glittering opulence verges on debauch. A dozen little bouquets of mimosa, dahlias, delphiniums, and scabious arvensis held in miniature crystal vases spring up amid a thicket of candlesticks that includes both vermeil Corinthian columns and "Rock Cut" crystal. Here and there vermeil apple boxes reflect the scene.

A rose-pink flowered chintz cloth with matching napkins establishes the dominant color for the place settings of "Framboise Rose" Tiffany Private Stock porcelain, "English King" vermeil flatware, "Honeycomb" cut crystal, and the classic individual "Bordeaux Bottle" Baccarat decanters designed, like the "Framboise Rose" porcelain, by Tiffany's Van Day Truex. Venetian glass baskets hold salt and pepper.

Mrs. Dudley's graceful white and gold lacquered Italian Regency chairs upholstered in rose moiré silk are from Rose Cumming, and her painted leather screen with its Chinoiserie motifs in the style of Pillement is from Florian Papp.

# DINNER
# BEFORE THE THEATER
*Mrs. Edward Byron Smith*

The bold and stylish patterns of "Old Imari" china set the tone of this pre-theater dinner table arranged by Chicago hostess Aleca Smith in her daughter's Fifth Avenue apartment.

The bare walls of the dining area provided a neutral backdrop for the posturing of a gilt wood Siamese dancer and the dominating bouquet of rubrum lilies set above the corner banquette. Small, irregularly placed cut-crystal cube vases keep colorful anemones close to the table, which is covered with an embroidered yellow linen organdy Porthault cloth. An imposing vermeil candelabrum gives the setting height, balancing the lilies and dancer. "Asian Rose" soup plates pick up the Imari colors. The flatware is "Shell and Thread" vermeil. The stemware is "Ariel." Two winsome "Bolognese" Meissen dogs join the party.

Before dinner the traditional caviar and champagne will be served while guests enjoy a spectacular view of the summer sunset over Central Park's reservoir. The iced caviar sits in a cut-crystal server. "Dom Pérignon" flutes stand beside a Swedish crystal champagne cooler. The plates are "Asian Rose," and two nineteenth-century silver pheasants animate the setting.

# CENTENNIAL
# ANNIVERSARY CELEBRATION
## *Mrs. James Hoban Harris*

Drawing on the formidable collection of family Tiffany silver originally presented to her father-in-law at his wedding in 1888, and acting on the well-founded principle that beautiful things of good report never fail to delight, Mrs. James Hoban Harris designs an anniversary celebration table. Her warm-toned and generously detailed setting is shot through with classic American charm.

The 1880s Tiffany silver, which includes "Chrysanthemum" flatware, a water pitcher, a covered vegetable dish, and two finely chased sauceboats holding flowers, is combined with "Dragon Sorrel" bone china and "Paris" Baccarat stemware.

Coffee is served from the sideboard in "Jardins Chinois" demitasse cups against the background of a painted Chinoiserie screen by Robert Crowder.

# ALL FOR ONE

---

Breakfast in Bed / Mario Buatta
Tropical Morning / Tiffany & Co.
TV Dinner / Mrs. Thomas L. Kempner
Dinner with Voltaire / Diana Vreeland
Dinner in Jail / Andy Warhol

---

# BREAKFAST IN BED

## *Mario Buatta*

On page 85 of Françoise Sagan's *Des Bleus à l'âme,* a favored character awakes "deposited on his back in the deliciously soft Porthault sheets" of his mistress.

Mme Sagan neglects in this image of indolence, wealth, and bland sensuality to tell her readers if his head was or was not resting on stacks of pillows or if his stuffed rabbit was nearby.

He might well awake here in the massed linens of this luxurious canopied bed—Porthault *en diable*—by Mario Buatta, America's presiding master of romantic decors.

His breakfast arrives on a round lacquered tray served on hand-painted "Oeillet Bleu" Chantilly porcelain. He will eat with Tiffany's "Bamboo" silver and pick at the morning mail from a wicker basket.

*Bonjour, paresse!*

# TROPICAL MORNING
## *Tiffany & Co.*

Nothing more civilized and elegant has yet been invented than the white canopy of a mosquito net in all its fragile, ephemeral simplicity; and what luxury is greater than having a wake-up cup of coffee brought to the bedside?

In this very grand and very simple French colonial scene, a French Empire campaign bed in polished iron lies under its white netting. A tropical plant and tropical flowers are held by a stoneware planter and vase by Erik Reiff. A blue, white, and brown "Ostindia" breakfast service is used with Tiffany's "Salem" flat silver.

The tablecloth is China Seas' "Oslo" cotton.

# TV DINNER
## *Mrs. Thomas L. Kempner*

---

The smooth movements of machines have played no small part in the look of contemporary interiors.

Here New York style-setter Nan Kempner gives a Sony KP-5000 projection TV a place of high prominence in this setting for a quiet dinner while awaiting guests invited for a glass of champagne.

Although the assertive TV demands and gets attention, Mrs. Kempner retakes possession of the space with overscaled objects and furniture.

Her TV tray set with a "Flora Danica" plate, "Shell and Thread" silver, and an "Ambassador" wineglass sits on the footstool of a commodious "Wicker-Wicker-Wicker" chaise by Michael Taylor, who also designed the skirted wicker table which Mrs. Kempner covers with an Yves Saint Laurent scarf and sets with Tiffany silver objects including a "Lily Pad" tray, "Honeycomb" and "Mock Orange" boxes, and a "Basket" dish.

A nineteenth-century Japanese vase holds plum blossoms beside a bronze Buddha.

Drawings by William Bailey, Henri Matisse, and Larry Rivers back the setting, and a gold-leaf Art Deco screen backs the TV.

To dine with the best company
To dine alone is impossible
To dine with my brilliant,
Audacious and totally remarkable
Friend is the best of company
Voltaire — Voltaire — Voltaire

# DINNER WITH VOLTAIRE
## *Diana Vreeland*

The "Empress of Fashion" in the guise of the Empress of Russia dines with Voltaire. "It's Catherine [the Great], not I, who is having dinner with her pen pal," Mrs. Vreeland explains. "There can be no candles, and only soft indirect light. I'm terrified of a table looking like breakfast is being served in the sunshine."

Although Voltaire and Catherine never met, their correspondence lasted sixteen years. Voltaire called her "the Semiramis of the Snows" and, when severely criticized by his friend and patron Frederick the Great for defending this superior but unscrupulous monarch, who was known to have precipitated the murders of her husband, Peter III, and his cousin Ivan to take the Russian throne, Voltaire simply replied, "One must love one's friends with all their faults."

Catherine in turn adored Voltaire, whom she described as "a great man who was very fond of me." She had many statues of him and once publicly curtsied to his bust and said, "There is the man to whom I owe all I know and all I am."

Mrs. Vreeland's white marble bust of Voltaire (courtesy of M. E. Hall, Jr.) is by the great French portrait sculptor Jean Antoine Houdon and carved around the time of Voltaire's death in 1778. Her porcelain pattern, "Flora Danica," was originally designed at Royal Copenhagen as a present to Catherine from the King of Denmark. "Windham" sterling silver flatware is placed on the right, following eighteenth-century Russian convention. A gloxinia sits in a brown earthenware cachepot beside Voltaire. Antique paisley shawls from Cherchez cover both the table and chair, which sit on a rare early-seventeenth-century Polonaise Kashan silk carpet from Stark.

# DINNER IN JAIL
## *Andy Warhol*

Andy Warhol made the Campbell's Soup can, the Brillo box, and the electric chair as familiar icons to art aficionados as "The Blue Boy," the "Giaconda," and "The Forge of Vulcan."

His sails are in every breeze; and if a trend's afoot, this maker of "superstars" and guru of the "glitterati" will have it photographed and interviewed and its portrait painted.

It was no surprise that, a few weeks after Warhol stated that a "dinner in jail" seemed "kind of appropriate because that's where so many of my friends are," *New York* magazine's 1980 New Year's issue announced that "weekends in jail really came into vogue during the seventies."

For Andy's dinner there is the traditional bread and water served with not so traditional Tiffany vermeil and crystal.

The diner amuses himself with Tiffany playing cards. There is a New York *Times* with articles about other people in jail, a bell to ring for reporters, and an Italian *fumetto*—always popular reading matter for the glitterati.

Friends have provided a personalized Tiffany sterling silver toothpaste tube key, and the cell itself is a work of modern art by Ronnie Cutrone.

# TÊTE-À-TÊTE

---

Dinner for Two / Cary Grant
Garden Party / Gloria Vanderbilt
Monday Night Football / Mrs. Alfred Bloomingdale
Dinner and a Show / Mark Hampton
Two for Lunch: Still Two for Dinner / Elsa Peretti
Regency Safari / Lee Radziwill
A Romantic Repast / Mrs. William Sarnoff
Soirée Intime / Mrs. Aileen Mehle (Suzy Knickerbocker)
Tête-à-Tête / MAC II
The Night Before Breakfast at Tiffany's / Dexter Design, Inc.
Gypsy Tearoom à la Tiffany / McMillen, Inc.
Matinee Day Lunch / Lionel Larner for Mia Farrow
Lunch for Two Writers on Long Island / Rosamond Bernier Russell
A Thousand and One Nights / The Honorable Joanne King Herring
Supper After Scheherazade / Mrs. Lawrence Copley Thaw
Christmas Eve / Tiffany & Co.
New Year's Eve / Tiffany & Co.

---

# DINNER
# FOR TWO

## *Cary Grant*

The view is Los Angeles; the wine is Californian; the colors are cool and bold; and the host—the host is the most debonair of film stars. He has played every character from the Mock Turtle to Cole Porter; and of course, since he first appeared on the screen in 1932 in *This Is the Night,* he has charmed legions of the most glamorous leading ladies.

Here on the terrace of his Beverly Hills home, Cary Grant stages a dinner for two. The air is one of good old straightforward romance with no nonsense about it. The message is still "This Is the Night."

The setting is smooth-surfaced and direct. The colonial purity of "Salem" silverware harmonizes with the rugged and irregular stripes of large-scale Tiffany inlaid earthenware plates.

A clump of spring flowers casually thrust into an "Ovalis" vase lends its serene and simple charm to the table, which is lit by crystal hurricanes.

Tiffany's "All-Purpose" wineglasses sum up the combination of utility and simple, pared-down elegance that Mr. Grant prefers.

# GARDEN PARTY
## *Gloria Vanderbilt*

---

If it can rightly be said that when we set the table we set the stage for a social performance, it can be said that few hostesses could be better equipped than Gloria Vanderbilt to bring to the art of table setting all the talents to make the performance a smash hit.

Artist; actress; author; designer of textiles, clothing, interiors, greeting cards, and stationery; and successful in all these diversely creative ventures, Miss Vanderbilt brings a happy combination of great style, quiet drama, invention, and professionalism to everything she undertakes.

In this garden setting, a graceful white gazebo defines the limits of a privileged and intimate dining spot. Ornate nineteenth-century shell-back wicker chairs from the Wicker Garden are placed as supporting actors in the evening's drama. The tablecloth with its brightly discreet little bouquets of flowers is designed by Miss Vanderbilt and very simply titled "Gloria." It gives a fresh foundation to "Coeur Fleurs," Tiffany Private Stock plates, "Tiffany Swag" goblets, "Audubon" vermeil flatware, and a fanciful collection of vermeil palm candlesticks, porcelain shell boxes, and a yellow Private Stock cachepot filled with the most demure daisies.

The title of this evening drama is unmistakably "Hearts and Flowers," but how it turns out is anyone's guess until the end of the third course.

# MONDAY NIGHT FOOTBALL
## *Mrs. Alfred Bloomingdale*

The deep-toned and richly detailed eighteenth-century English Chippendale table and chairs, anchored by a carved and gilded leather screen, in the Bloomingdales' Holmby Hills library set a very civilized tone for this fanciful football dinner for two.

"Alfred dislikes eating on a tray—so on football nights the TV comes to dinner at the library table," says Betsy Bloomingdale.

The portable TV becomes an ornamental object, and one of no small elegance when surrounded by the Bloomingdales' hand-painted Tiffany "Carrousel Chinois" Private Stock porcelain, "King William" silver flatware, classically paneled "Metternich" crystal stemware, and an intricately hand-wrought reproduction of an eighteenth-century French silver tureen. Three heights of "Rock Cut" crystal candlesticks give light and balance. Pink nerine lilies float airily above orange day lilies and echeverias sprouting from silver jiggers. Victorian ivory-handled fish forks and knives lend their own eclectic charm. The jiggers used as vases and snake paperweights converted to napkin rings lend a note of surprise and whimsy that contributes to the bright air of mixed good fun and well-being that Betsy Bloomingdale brings in abundance to all her table settings.

# DINNER
# AND A SHOW
## *Mark Hampton*

Young New York designer Mark Hampton is noted for mixing a fresh wit with an informed, conservative taste.

Here a couple will dine on the diagonal in a small sitting room smartly furnished with black and gold lacquers, including a striking eighteenth-century cabinet holding the television set and a pair of Chinese nineteenth-century tables holding lilacs and peonies.

Both will eat with "Hamilton" vermeil flatware from "Dragon Sorrel" porcelain and drink from flared crystal wineglasses and diamond-cut water tumblers. Individual "Dionysis" decanters, their crystal stoppers replaced by ordinary corks, sit on the individual brass and glass low tables—red for him, white for her. If his conversation fails to be as disarming and animated as Mark Hampton's, she will watch TV.

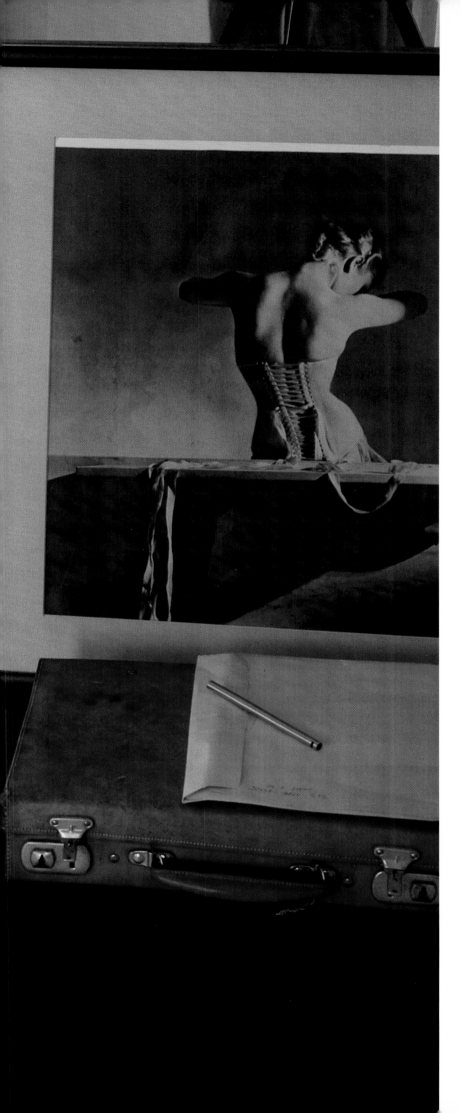

# TWO FOR LUNCH:
## *Elsa Peretti*

There can be no doubt that Elsa Peretti, more than any other designer, has created the look of contemporary jewelry with her "Peretti Bean," her "Open Heart," her "Diamonds by the Yard," and her many, many other inventive, sculptural designs for Tiffany's.

Here she turns her able and knowing hand to "things for the home," as she puts it, and a whole new era of twentieth-century objects begins.

An early Horst fashion photo sits on the file cabinet beside her New York "work" table cleared for lunch and set with her hand-blown crystal plates and bowl whose crystal "Pot Cover" doubles as an ashtray. Flat silver is "Rat Tail," and the wineglass is "All-Purpose," as is the food.

79

# STILL TWO
# FOR DINNER

Dinner moves to a low table before the open hearth. The fire and the candles held in two Peretti "Bone" candlesticks, one in crystal and one in silver, light the simple meal of baked potatoes, caviar, and champagne followed by fresh strawberries. The flat silver and plates continue in service from lunch. The flutes are "Dom Pérignon," like the champagne. Caviar is held in the tasseled lid of a silver Peretti pumpkin. The black jade cigarette holder, the silver "Pot Cover" ashtray, and the silver dishes holding strawberries are all designed by Elsa Peretti.

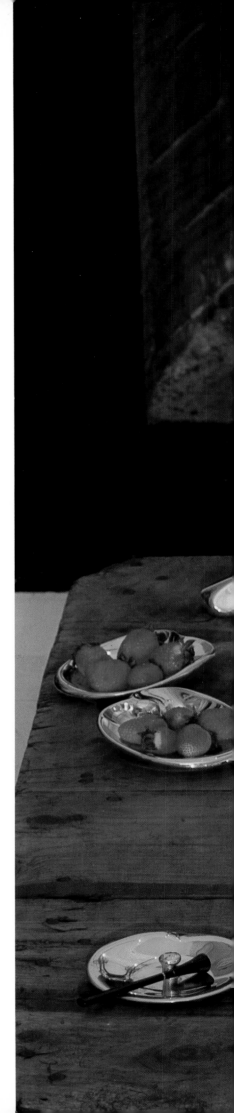

# REGENCY SAFARI
## *Lee Radziwill*

Relaxed and royal Bengal tigers cavort in a painting by J. L. Agasse and lend their stripes to the silk velvet upholstery at this seductive dinner for two, where Lee Radziwill not only revisits the light and hardy styles of Regency England but reawakes as well its studied hedonism and exotic "oriental" fancies.

The velvet skirted table has ample Tiffany vermeil, cut crystal, and candlelight. It centers on an onyx egg held by a golden bangle.

A pair of French Art Deco bronze giraffes by Wheeler Williams cast their gently curious eyes on the setting based on a *faux* marble painted floor by Robert Jackson.

# A ROMANTIC REPAST

## *Mrs. William Sarnoff*

The monarchical decor of the Hapsburg court, its red velvets, its white satins, its gold laces and embroideries, and its jewels, are recalled by Mrs. William Sarnoff in this intimate dinner whose multiple richness of elements burgeons with the romance of things past.

Mrs. Sarnoff's state portrait by the court painter Winterhalter of the beautiful young Princess Elizabeth of Hungary and the Two Sicilies sets the tone. Colors are restricted to the Hapsburgs' red and white. An antique gold lace scarf from Mrs. Sarnoff's family decorates the satin-covered table set with "Chrysanthemum" vermeil turned down in the European fashion, gold and white "Sheffield" bone china, "Antoinette" cut crystal, and Royal Berlin birds. A leaf-shaped vermeil *ravier* holds a ruby and diamond ring tied into pearl lariats, all by Tiffany jewelry designer Angela Cummings and all reminiscent of the jewels worn by the Princess Elizabeth in her portrait. Black lacquer side tables hold a bouquet of red silk flowers and a nineteenth-century black lacquer birdcage.

There are wine and roses and candlelight, and Viennese waltzes in the background.

# SOIRÉE INTIME

## *Mrs. Aileen Mehle (Suzy Knickerbocker)*

The feuds and "non-feuds," the intrigues and the celebrations of the chic, the talented, the glittering, the lovely, the wonderful, the adorable, and the "grande" are set aside by "Suzy," the prima diva of syndicated columnists, for an intimate supper at home.

Awash in candlelight, the richly detailed Louis XV salon takes on an allure of "opera opulence" and romance.

Rose-bodied "Sakai" china keeps harmony with the interior's golden tones. The vermeil flatware is "English King." There is "Honeycomb" cut crystal for wine and champagne, and an eighteenth-century French gilt bronze and crystal candelabrum to light the jubilantly luxurious table for two.

# TÊTE-À-TÊTE
## *MAC II*

---

The contented self-confidence of Victorian times was nowhere more evident than in the lush invention of nineteenth-century table settings. Tables lavishly dressed in "silencers," underskirts, and lace cloths; tables laden with silver and crystal; compotes piled high with formal architectures of fruits and flowers; geysers of greenery; the burnishing glimmer of candlelight: all took part in making the Victorian table a most remarkable achievement of Western culture.

With all the romance and delight in excess of La Belle Epoque, Mica Ertegun and Chessy Rayner of MAC II create an intimate dinner for two in a small pavilion, lace-lined and tented in dark green silk.

Papier-mâché chairs inlaid with mother-of-pearl face a table skirted in silk to match the pavilion and covered in antique lace.

Timeless "Drabware" service plates hold individual silver tureens with cane-wrapped handles. Flat silver is "King William." There are heavy-stemmed "Victoria" wineglasses and silver beakers. A low silver compote foots the central pyramid of fresh strawberries. There are orchids and candlelight and a very civilized air of well-being.

# THE NIGHT BEFORE
# BREAKFAST AT TIFFANY'S

*Dexter Design, Inc.*

# MATINEE DAY LUNCH

## *Lionel Larner for Mia Farrow*

Top theater and film agent Lionel Larner lives in a sun-and-art-filled Upper East Side Manhattan penthouse surrounded by terrace gardens and brimming over with his own English charm. Here he enjoys transforming business meetings with his "stars," who include Glenda Jackson, Mia Farrow, Diana Rigg, Anne Baxter, and Carroll O'Connor, into thoroughly delightful private entertainments.

"Athlone" yellow and gold china set on a blue and white Souleiado country print from Pierre Deux, baluster stemware, antique Tiffany flat silver, and a "Dionysis" decanter were his choice for this between-performances matinee day lunch with Mia Farrow during her run in *Romantic Comedy*.

The atmosphere is cosmopolitan but thoroughly relaxed. Giacometti lamps flank seventeenth-century Italian landscape paintings behind the setting which includes a limestone statue of a "Bather" by Bernard Reder and a simple bunch of anemones in a contemporary Tiffany engraved glass vase.

The anemones are repeated by the Matisse painting hanging over a marble-topped Louis XVI console where the paneled silver coffee service and a silver bowl of fresh fruit wait beside a seated figure by José de Creeft.

# LUNCH FOR TWO WRITERS ON LONG ISLAND

## *Rosamond Bernier Russell*

Rosamond Bernier Russell, popular lecturer on arts and artists, television interviewer, friend of almost every major figure active in the art, music, literature, and design of our times, and for many years the guiding spirit and editor of *L'Oeil* magazine, knows probably as much about the ins and outs of eighteenth-, nineteenth-, and twentieth-century culture as anyone—with the possible exception of the New York *Times* art critic John Russell, who is, of course, her husband and frequent collaborator.

Here, before the backdrop of Jasper Johns's magistral 1976 print "Corpse and Mirror" (a gift of their friend the artist), they lunch at a small round table covered in a green and pink paisley French country print from Pierre Deux and sit on straight-backed Louis XIII country side chairs with pale green box cushions.

With lectures, articles, and television scripts to prepare there is little time for flower arranging, so an intriguing centerpiece has been constructed from the uneven forms of natural crystals in a variety of muted colors.

"Fleurettes" Tiffany Private Stock plates with their smooth, intense blue backgrounds gain control of the setting's many patterns. The silver is "Rat Tail," and wines from the simplest of carafes will be served in late-seventeenth-century Augsburg beakers.

Conversation will be as highly civilized and as fresh and intricately textured as this delightful table.

# A THOUSAND AND ONE NIGHTS

## *The Honorable Joanne King Herring*

The joyously relentless elaboration and sumptuous theatricality of Joanne Herring's fanciful setting conjure up all the princely splendors of Morocco and Pakistan combined. And well they should. Mrs. Herring is Honorary Consul to both countries and works to promote their flourishing arts and crafts industries.

Here in her Houston home she delights in combining decorative objects that she frankly admits "others might not consider glamorous" but which bring "vitality, spontaneity, and zest" to entertainments.

Among Mrs. Herring's mirrored embroideries and ceramic menagerie, the table includes "Black Shoulder" Tiffany Private Stock porcelain, "Olympian" flatware, "Old Galway" crystal goblets, and a vermeil "Honeycomb" box.

The exoticism is worthy of an Adah Isaacs Menken extravaganza, and that queen of the nineteenth-century stage might comfortably lounge here in full princely regalia, reciting her inimitable lines:

"Decked in jewels and lace, I laugh beneath the
gas-light's glare, and quaff the purple wine."

# SUPPER AFTER SCHEHERAZADE
## *Mrs. Lawrence Copley Thaw*

---

Somewhere in the *Arabian Nights*, King Shahriyar's beautiful young wife Scheherazade must have described a mosaic table of lapis lazuli, malachite, and colored marbles set with vermeil, strewn with gold and jeweled boxes, ornamented with orchids, and guarded by two golden monkeys.

In the spirit of Léon Bakst, whose costumes and sets for Diaghilev's Ballets Russes production of *Scheherazade* revolutionized early-twentieth-century design, New York hostess and ballet supporter Lee Thaw sets a magnificent early-nineteenth-century Italian mosaic table with "Audubon" vermeil flatware, gadrooned vermeil service plates, "Metternich" champagne flutes, and cut-crystal vodka glasses. Tiffany jewelry designer Jean Schlumberger's gold and diamond "Wings" cigarette case and his smaller "Melon," "Starfish," and "Peapod" gold boxes sit about the table. A vermeil "King Cole" mug, remade by Tiffany's from its original late 1890s dies, holds a variety of orchids. The attendant monkeys are also in Tiffany vermeil.

There are blinis and caviar. Chairs are draped with a remarkable collection of nineteenth-century Bokhara ikats from Russian Turkestan.

"This," Mrs. Thaw explains, "is all absurdly, outrageously grand and just the way we are *not* going to live."

# CHRISTMAS EVE
## *Tiffany & Co.*

Tiffany's yellow stags sit in as reindeer at this extravagant, candlelit dinner for two worthy of Louis Comfort Tiffany himself, whose favorite color was yellow and whose favored life-style was extravagance.

There is ample caviar in cut-crystal servers sitting on yellow "Nevers" plates. Wine waits to be poured into "Saga" stemware from "Celestial" decanters. The silver is "Chrysanthemum," and table linens are made from Vice Versa's "Byzantium."

As Her devotion is expressed in this warm-toned and rich-textured setting (clearly masterminded by no ordinary force), His devotion is expressed by the magnificent diamond loop necklace modeled by their stag and the pearl choker that spills out of a "Chelsea Sunflower" dish to show off its extraordinary yellow cabochon sapphire and diamond clasp.

Both jewels are, of course, by Tiffany designer Angela Cummings.

# NEW YEAR'S EVE

## *Tiffany & Co.*

Only restraint would be inappropriate at a time of mixed resolution, sentimentality, and celebration when decors and decorum can run self-confidently from the rich and riotous to the frivolous and erratic.

Here, in this New Year's Eve dinner setting, the most diverse styles participate in gilt and glittering harmony.

If there are pervasive echoes of the Napoleonic era in the furniture and in the neoclassic patterns of the "Palmette" bone china dinner service and in the "Directoire" Private Stock dessert plates, there is more than a hint of Victorianism in the "Halcyon" vase filled with antique Chinese gilt wood lotuses and in the side table covered with a nineteenth-century flowered Bessarabian carpet. The eighteenth century is represented by "English King" vermeil flatware and white Berlin porcelain birds, and the twentieth by the "Artichoke" vase, "Honeycomb" box, "Riyadh" bowl, and "Bamboo" candlesticks included in the collection of Tiffany vermeil.

The crystal stemware is "Metternich," and the spots of Brunschwig's silk velvet "Leopard" upholstery are picked up by Private Stock coffee cups.

# MORNING

---

Breakfast with Houseguests / Mr. and Mrs. James Stewart
Breakfast in Cuernavaca / Tiffany & Co.
Primavera / John Saladino
A Family Country Breakfast / Mrs. John R. Drexel III
A Connecticut Hunt Breakfast / Mrs. William F. Buckley, Jr.
Christmas Morning / Tiffany & Co.

---

# BREAKFAST
# WITH HOUSEGUESTS
## *Mr. and Mrs. James Stewart*

Our slow-speaking, right-thinking, all-around-American film hero James Stewart is probably best remembered for his role as the invisible rabbit Harvey's genial alcoholic friend.

The Stewarts, since *Harvey*, have befriended animals in general. They support and travel yearly to the wildlife preserves of East Africa, and Gloria Stewart sits on the board of the Los Angeles Zoo.

The decoration of their Beverly Hills house includes animal paintings and sculptures of every size, shape, and attitude, and it comes as no surprise to guests in the Stewarts' sunny green and yellow breakfast room to find Harvey invited to the table and joined by a merry farmyard contingent of pigs, cows, and a flowered duck, all in brightly painted ceramic, cavorting about a bowl piled with products of the Stewarts' flourishing garden.

The room's outdoor feeling, with its bamboo lattice motifs, is carried through with "Bamboo" flat silver, "Bamboo" glasses for tomato juice, and the freshly colored oriental landscapes of "Chinese Green Willow" dishes.

The accent at the Stewarts' table is always on good food in reasonable quantities, as much of it home-grown as possible.

The Stewarts, however, do not keep bees, so the pot of home-produced honey was brought by a friend, Henry Fonda.

# BREAKFAST
# IN CUERNAVACA
## *Tiffany & Co.*

The classic pine and pigskin "equipal" chairs; the wrought-iron window grille; the heavy moldings of Spanish Colonial woodwork; a climbing geranium in its hand-thrown terra-cotta pot; the dazzling sunshine—they all say Mexico.

In the dining room of the Cuernavaca Racquet Club, surrounded by its vast acreage of well-manicured tropical paradise, the breakfast table is set in muted pinks and oranges. The spare, sturdy forms and sensual surface of gray/pink American "Peach Bloom" stoneware contrast with a subtle gradation of dominant orange tones: the freshly cut melons, the pale peach Porthault table linen, and the crystal pitcher filled with fresh Mexican orange juice. The flat silver is Tiffany's "Bamboo," and local breakfast breads are served from a sterling silver basket woven in Mexico especially for Tiffany & Co.

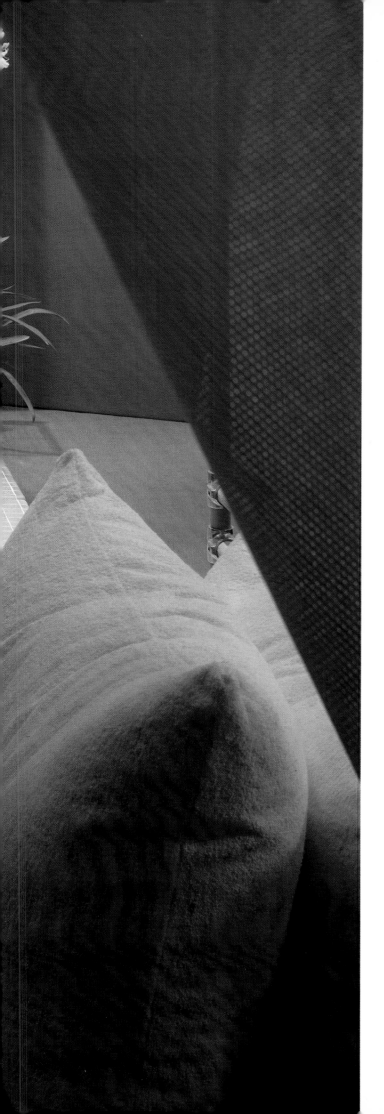

# PRIMAVERA
## *John Saladino*

Vegetables and vitamins are served up in an atmosphere of health, high tech, and high spirits by New York designer John Saladino.

In this pared-down interior every detail is sleek and slim, from the exercise mats to the steel industrial shelving that serves for both buffet and table. Transparent side tables were made by inverting Tiffany's crystal flower tubs. The cool and understated tile floor coordinates with "Celadon" porcelain. There is unornamented Tiffany silver everywhere, and guests can check their measurements with a sterling silver tape measure.

# A FAMILY
# COUNTRY BREAKFAST
## *Mrs. John R. Drexel III*

"I suppose everyone expects me to do a dinner, which is all very well," says leading Newport hostess Noreen Drexel, "but my favorite meal has always been breakfast, a big breakfast in the kitchen with my whole family, including my grandchildren—with real brown bread and real brown eggs in wicker baskets, and English muffins."

For this cozy family breakfast, full to overflowing with English charm in its every detail, Mrs. Drexel achieves her preferred country kitchen feeling with a varied collection of English transfer ware in small-scale, all-over floral motifs. The mix of blue "Liberty," "Green Velvet," and "Pink Velvet" dishes with Laura Ashley print table linens has that happily illogical but admirable and disarming confusion of pattern of which the English since Victorian times so well know the secret.

Miniature Paddington Bears and Peter Rabbit mugs mark the children's places. A yellow Paris porcelain cow shares a dresser shelf with a white Nymphenburg hippopotamus in honor of one of Mrs. Drexel's grandsons, nicknamed "Hippo."

# A CONNECTICUT HUNT BREAKFAST

## Mrs. William F. Buckley, Jr.

The main courtyard teems with horses and foxhounds. The hunters in their pink jackets are about to descend on the "breakfast." The foundations of this rite are tradition itself, and with her habitual exuberance, Pat Buckley gives the setting imaginative and eminently stylish opulence.

There is blatant grandeur in the heroically scaled Japanese Imari plates, and wit in the cobalt-blue porcelain boxes used as salts and peppers. Both are played off against the backdrop of a monumental seventeenth-century Flemish still life, "After the Day's Sport" by Jan Fyt, from Wildenstein & Company.

The shift in scale from such jewel-like details as the porcelain boxes to the oversized plates, with their quiet little quail nestling in the grass, gives a very special panache to this hearty hunt breakfast.

On the Jacobean gateleg oval oak table Mrs. Buckley places blue and ocher "Ostindia" stoneware with covered soup bowls, "English King" flatware, and generously scaled baluster-stemmed crystal goblets. The centerpiece of a large silver platter laden with fresh fruits and flanked by silver tankard pitchers repeats the seventeenth-century still-life theme.

Cakes, nuts, and coffee wait on the sideboard to be served from a sterling silver service. The coffee will be in "Gloucester Blue" finestone mugs.

# CHRISTMAS MORNING
## *Tiffany & Co.*

Horn furniture is an obligatory feature of German hunting lodges, just as ornamented pine trees are an obligatory feature of German Christmas decorations. Both became stylish in England shortly after the young English Queen, Victoria, married her German cousin Prince Albert of Saxe-Coburg in 1840; and both arrived soon after in America, to become as American as teddy bears and cranberry muffins.

Recapturing a Victorian Christmas that could well have taken place at Victoria's Balmoral Castle or Teddy Roosevelt's Sagamore Hill, Tiffany's has assembled a collection of horn furniture and even a horn chandelier. Boxes of gifts, including a "Bacchus" Flask made from 1880s Tiffany patterns, Quimper plates, and an Este coffee set, are scattered everywhere about the room, which features an antique Bessarabian flowered kilim from Doris Leslie Blau of the type so popular in Victorian times, a grandly proportioned chesterfield sofa, and a romantic mid-nineteenth-century American painting that carries on the nostalgic tone of the setting.

Breakfast dishes are the typically Victorian "Mandarin" pattern, and an antique "Japanese Revival"-style silver Tiffany punch bowl made in 1880 holds bright red apples. Amaryllis bloom in earthenware cachepots, and a teddy bear sits in a miniature steer-horn chair. The muffins in the silver "Monteith" bowl, used here as a breadbasket, are naturally cranberry.

# NOON

---

Lunch for Two / Mrs. Henry Kissinger
A Small In-office Lunch / John T. Sargent
A Client Lunch at Wells, Rich, Greene, Inc. / Mrs. Harding Lawrence
A Thai Terrace Lunch / Mr. and Mrs. Tony Duquette
Déjeuner Normand / Prince and Princess Edouard de Lobkowicz
For Julia Child and Company / Julia Child
Connecticut Sunday Lunch / Angela Cummings
Country Buffet at Templeton / C. Z. Guest
Lunch in a Loft / John Loring
Lunch in the Corporate Boardroom / Letitia Baldrige
First Birthday / Lorna de Wangen

---

# LUNCH FOR TWO
## *Mrs. Henry Kissinger*

Chinese design is informed by a pure, natural nobility and grace, and Western craftsmen have liberally borrowed the simple vigor of its lines and the sustained sobriety of its quietly rich colors for over three hundred years.

In this engagingly stylish and low-keyed setting by Nancy Kissinger, the blackwood table and chairs are from eighteenth-century Peking. The sparsely decorated stonewares recall the tranquil beauty of Sung dishes. Plates are by Tennessee potter Nancy Lamb, who trained at "The Royal" in Copenhagen, and bowls are by Erik Reiff, Royal Copenhagen's master craftsman. Silver is Tiffany's "Salem."

The exceptional eighteenth-century Peking carpet from William Coury which echoes the enduring patterns of Greek and Roman pavements is of a type favored by the greatest of Chinese rulers, the K'ang-hsi Emperor, a gentleman who would undoubtedly have found this setting totally to his liking.

# A SMALL IN-OFFICE LUNCH

## *John T. Sargent*

The single most important feature of the executive office lunch is not the food and not the setting in itself but rather the assurance that both will be pleasant and that neither will obtrude on the business at hand.

Here John Sargent, Chairman of the Board of Doubleday, awaits three associates in his Manhattan office.

The handsome and straightforward place settings echo the room's collection of ornamental Chinese objects with the Chinoiserie motifs of "Si Kiang" porcelain. "King William" silver and "St. Rémy" glasses are both simple classics. The table centers on a Monteith bowl filled with green Anjou pears. There are small individual "Sparta" crystal ashtrays with Doubleday matches for the guests and a larger ashtray for Mr. Sargent's habitual cigar.

From a table across the room, Jo Davidson's bust of Somerset Maugham, who was of course a Doubleday author, watches over the coffee service.

# A CLIENT LUNCH
# AT WELLS, RICH, GREENE, INC.

## *Mrs. Harding Lawrence*

Mary Wells Lawrence has an unusual flair for combining business with pleasant elegance. Here, at a lunch for clients in the setting of her Houston office, she designs a table with the quick wit and polish she brings to the world of advertising.

There is a sober luxury to the setting of flowered and fretted "Jardin de Jade" Tiffany Private Stock plates combined with "Bamboo" sterling flatware, silver tumblers, and heavy-stemmed crystal goblets all on a yellow-and-white-striped tablecloth.

Guests are reminded of Mrs. Lawrence's noted clients by their products, which include Alka-Seltzer packets at each place, a Bic pen and lighter, and "Benson & Hedges" engraved on a silver cigarette box.

On the sideboard, more clients are represented by soft drinks and a juice extractor, while pinned-up panels block out a future commercial.

The quiet plain-weave patterns of the sisal mat wall covering, the rattan cane chairs, and the ornamental basket centerpiece give a note of oriental tranquillity to the setting.

# A THAI TERRACE LUNCH

*Mr. and Mrs. Tony Duquette*

When Shangri-La is discovered, its governing sorcerer's table will be of greenest malachite surrounded by malachite chairs and little Siamese spirit houses hiding in the lush neighboring jungle. Flanked by "Rat Tail" silver, spinach-green imperial "Chinese Tigers" will cavort about the luncheon plates. Cooling drinks will be poured from a golden pineapple pitcher; and, while giant tropical blossoms fall from sheltering trees, throaty green-mouthed cypripedium orchids will survey the scene with the beautifully cool indifference of insects content to leave a first course of the pinkest of shrimp to mere mortals.

The credits will list the designer as none other than Tony Duquette, Hollywood's master of visual storytelling, who brings to every setting the vitality and freshness of his truly spectacular imagination.

# DÉJEUNER NORMAND
## *Prince and Princess Edouard de Lobkowicz*

At the late-eighteenth-century manor house of Ujezd in western Normandy the Prince and Princess Lobkowicz prepare for a winter weekend luncheon.

The round table is set for eight with "Dioraflor" porcelain and family silver and drenched in the clear cool light of the Norman countryside so beloved by French Impressionists.

The nineteenth-century Meissen centerpiece, which the Princess has surrounded with pine branches, depicts hounds somewhat unsuccessfully attacking a wild boar. It contrasts amusingly with demure little bouquets of bright blue and yellow primroses.

A large seventeenth-century painting of exotic birds by Paul de Vos hangs over the marbleized wood side table. The room also contains an equestrian portrait of Françoise de Lobkowicz's ancestor Louis XIV.

# FOR JULIA CHILD AND COMPANY

*Julia Child*

When the day comes that each and every American is an accomplished gourmet cook, all credit will be due to Julia Child and her dedication to teaching servantless America "the enjoyment of producing something wonderful to eat."

Here in her Cambridge home, surrounded by the vigorous forms of her battery of pots, pans, ladles, strainers, kettles, and casseroles, she sets the kitchen's sturdy oak table with French country-print linens from Pierre Deux in Boston, "American Stoneware," bugle glasses, and "Rat Tail" flatware. Stoneware bowls overflowing with fresh fruits and vegetables provide all the decoration that will be needed for this meal whose lusty and abundant culinary riches would be ornament enough for any table.

# CONNECTICUT SUNDAY LUNCH
## *Angela Cummings*

Jewels are part of daily life for Tiffany designer Angela Cummings. It comes, then, as no surprise to discover a fistful of citrines mixed in with the shafts of afternoon sunshine that stream through stone-mullioned Tudor windows and scatter themselves across the table of her Connecticut home.

With an extraordinary eye for colors and natural form, Miss Cummings decorates her tables with whatever the season and nature provide. Here, on a mid-autumn afternoon, she fills brown lusterware jars with flaming maple leaves and bright little sprigs of wild berries, bringing the outdoors in with the sunshine.

Colors are kept autumnal throughout. The pale topaz wine in a handsome crystal pitcher; the white butter plates loaded with crusty home-baked breads; the rich tobacco-brown shoulders encrusted with gold-ringed almond-green cabochons of the Tiffany Private Stock hors d'oeuvre plates: they all have their say about the good things of New England country life, its natural charm, and the warmth of its hospitality.

The natural-wood country table surrounded by a splendid set of Chippendale chairs with elaborately interlaced splats and ball-and-claw cabriole legs, the pistol-handled "Rat Tail" flat silver, the bugle-shaped wineglasses, the plain white Wedgwood dinner plates, the warm-toned antique Persian Herez carpet all show a detailed understanding of New England tradition and manners.

# COUNTRY BUFFET
# AT TEMPLETON
## *C. Z. Guest*

Whether the subject is horses, gardening, style, or the vicissitudes of society, C. Z. Guest is at home and on top of the situation, always a leader, always contributing her own imaginative and sensible point of view.

Her patrician love of horses, the country, and all things English is reflected in this buffet at Templeton, her house at Old Westbury, Long Island.

"Going to the Fair," a delightful horse painting by nineteenth-century American artist Henry Van Ingen, hangs above the lavishly appointed Hepplewhite sideboard buffet where one of Winston Guest's many polo trophies, the Indian Polo Association Annual Championship Challenge Cup, is surrounded by desserts.

Other polo trophies, such as the silver cigar box presented to Mr. Guest in 1939 when he played on the winning American Team in the International Championships, sit on the tables.

Each table, set for four, is covered in Clarence House's "Brighton" English chintz and set with "Sakai" porcelain, "Flemish" silver, and engraved crystal mugs.

Not only does C. Z. Guest write extensively on flowers and gardening, the orchids she grows at her Palm Beach house are legendary; and here, too, at Templeton there are orchids everywhere.

# LUNCH IN A LOFT

*John Loring*

The arts and crafts are clearly alive and about to be well fed at this SoHo table, which speaks to us of aestheticism in deliberately muted tones. There are echoes of the epicurian antics of New York's art world mixed with the poetic refinements of Sung Dynasty stoneware.

The colors are studied. Artichokes in full bloom pick up the dominant blue of a lyrical abstraction by New York painter David Diao. Sage-green napkins quietly contrast with the terra-cotta cloth (both of Brunschwig & Fils' "Yalis Chintz"). The low-key, natural scale of grays, gray-greens, beiges, and earth tones are accented by the pale acidic green of the Anjou pears and the citrine yellow of the wine.

The table is set with Tiffany's own "Vermont" crackle-glaze hand-thrown stoneware around a center bowl made for Tiffany's by Royal Copenhagen's master potter Erik Reiff; both are inspired by late Sung models. The silver is "Salem," turned down in the European fashion. "Antik" garland-etched, tumbler-shaped wineglasses carry on European table-setting convention and contribute to the table's relaxed formality.

The sideboard, designed in the 1920s by Gilbert Rhode for Herman Miller, holds covered "Vermont" serving dishes, beside exotic flowers arranged in a set of three basic "Tiffany Cylinder" vases of sand-glaze American earthenware designed by Mr. Loring.

# LUNCH IN THE
# CORPORATE BOARDROOM
## *Letitia Baldrige*

Letitia Baldrige, a director of four corporate boards, sets a lunch in the boardroom of the New York Bank for Savings, using octagonal oriental serving platters for luncheon plates.

Instead of sitting at the traditional table, this bank's trustees (Ms. Baldrige included) sit in comfortable swivel chairs in front of teak and chrome versions of the old school desk.

Breadsticks fit nicely in the pencil trays, silver beakers are used for the wine, and bud vases hold silver pens and pencils.

Oversized napkins in Imari colors repeat the colors of the plates; the sterling flatware is "King William."

The accessories are simple and contemporary in feeling—the butter plates are actually ashtrays. Each desk is set with a miniature silver ice bucket planted with an aloe plant.

# FIRST BIRTHDAY
## *Lorna de Wangen*

---

Big occasion—little guests.

Lorna de Wangen fills this First Birthday party with the bright-colored spirals and zigzags that children's eyes like best.

The revelers will each sit in a Victorian high chair set with silver baby pusher, fork, spoon, and cup. The birthday girl has been presented with a silver alphabet plate and rattle.

"Emma," the family maid sculpted by Carol Anthony, brings in the cake, which will be eaten off multicolor "Crackle" Tiffany Private Stock plates.

There are jelly beans in Tiffany heart boxes and a tub of presents sitting on the confetti-spotted tablecloth.

# NIGHT

---

Dinner with Your Best Friend / Françoise de la Renta
Triangle / Ruben de Saavedra
A Timeless Table / Van Day Truex
Supper with Arthur Smith / Arthur Smith
Dîner: Rouge et Noir / Lily Auchincloss
Food for Thought / Robert Currie and Christine Maly
Dinner for Four / Angelo Donghia
Dinner / Douglas Fairbanks, Jr.
Country Supper on the Back Porch / Mrs. Angier Biddle Duke
Heart to Heart / Mrs. Donald Newhouse
Exposure / Mrs. John Murchison
Formally Informal Wine Cellar Supper / Mrs. James D. Robinson, Jr.
At Home on the Avenue / Mrs. Seymour Berkson

---

# DINNER WITH
# YOUR BEST FRIEND

## *Françoise de la Renta*

---

La Belle Époque gave in to every decorative impulse. As feeling overcame reason in the late nineteenth century, architecture succumbed to ornament, and life was played for every milligram of romance, emotion, and sentiment that could be wrested from it against background decors of sumptuous detail and charming irregularity of style.

Françoise de la Renta, long the guiding spirit of French *Vogue*, has adopted the styles of La Belle Epoque as her own, infused them with her untiring vitality and explosive enthusiasm, and again and again interpreted them with pyrotechnic panache.

What matter if, as one contemporary critic said of this high-eclectic style, things are "not strongly Greek or strongly Gothic," if the classic key designs of the Greek Revival chairs from Didier Aaron have little to do with the Gothic Revival quatrefoils, crosses, and fleurs-de-lis of the needlepoint carpet from Stark, or if unruly pineapples have replaced flowers on the curious American Empire table set with "Halcyon" Private Stock plates, "Double Diamond" stemware, and "Rat Tail" silver.

The background painting is titled "Jour de Fête" and there is an incomparable air of anticipation, excitement, and festivity about this small dinner for a couple with their best friend, stylishly transformed by Mme de la Renta to an event of no small importance.

# TRIANGLE
## *Ruben de Saavedra*

The asymmetric arrangement, the uneven number, the oblique line—all animate interior design, and Ruben de Saavedra calls on them all in this suave and unexpected setting that calmly breaks every rule of classic arrangement.

The sleek geometrics of Tiffany's "Black on Black" pottery sit in a black-lacquered interior lit by the broken reflections of "Rock Cut" crystal candlesticks. There is plentiful silver, including "Salem" flatware and ice-filled can pitchers holding champagne. The designer has taken black as the dominant color and explored its broad and varied possibilities to great effect.

A plump Boterro bronze pug dog, superb and disquieting, sits in the midst of this contemporary field of dramatic action.

# A TIMELESS TABLE
## *Van Day Truex*

Tiffany's long-time design director Van Day Truex would often say, "Mother Nature, she's always the best designer." He borrowed liberally the patterns and forms of her fruits and flowers, her leaves and plants, her seed pods, her shells, and her abstract honeycomb or crystal structures. Her quiet natural earth colors were his constant favorites.

Here he arranges a handsome and unashamedly stylish table for one of the small dinners he loved to cook and enjoy with a few privileged friends.

"Palermo" and "Contessa" brown-and-gold-rimmed porcelain, used with "Hamilton" vermeil and "All-Purpose" wineglasses, sits on a natural beige cloth of textured cotton. The chairs, whose design is inspired by Jean-Michel Frank, a friend of Truex's student days in Paris, are Bielecky Brothers' wrapped cane classics.

There is a simple centerpiece of natural shells. There are no flowers, no candles to interfere with the conversation, which will center on "the provocative, the intellectual, the brilliant, the creative."

159

# SUPPER WITH ARTHUR SMITH
## *Arthur Smith*

---

Among the most significant design discoveries of the late seventies and beginning of the eighties are the works of Jean-Michel Frank and Émile Jacques Ruhlmann, Eileen Gray and Suë et Mare, of Décorchemont, René Lalique, and Jean Dunand, the masters of 1920s French Art Deco.

Young New York designer Arthur Smith has been a leader in the revival of these great artist/craftsmen.

With a strikingly spare and luxurious setting of "Black Shoulder" porcelain, "Audubon" vermeil, and "All-Purpose" wineglasses based on a pedestal table of his own invention, he uses a splendid set of Jean-Michel Frank dining room chairs and a masterful screen by Eileen Gray constructed of irregular cork-covered panels.

Constantin Brancusi's brass sculpture "Sleeping Muse" acts as a centerpiece.

# DÎNER:
# ROUGE ET NOIR
## *Lily Auchincloss*

Few hostesses are so acutely aware of the "look of the times" as Lily Auchincloss. Through her daily work as active Trustee of the Museum of Modern Art she joins with art and design in all its newest and finest guises.

Her table settings reflect her long-standing association with modernism—no prints, no patterns, no floral elaborations, no "decorator" pastel colors. There are boldness, simplicity, and eminent stylishness in her use of basic forms and primary colors, mixed with an animated play of light across refracting, reflecting, and thoroughly modern surfaces.

"A red lacquer table is really my trademark," she states. "I like a 'shiny' festive look and to use things that aren't flowers as centerpieces—mercury glass or cut-crystal candlesticks—but the main thing is no flowers and no patterns!—and no water glasses, and no soup plates! —You can't build a meal on a lake, can you!"

The dominant black and red spiral of her dining room's Alexander Calder tapestry is directly echoed by the stainless-steel and red-lacquer pedestal table designed for Lily Auchincloss by John Bedenkapp and set with oversized "Black on Black" earthenware plates by Tiffany potter Mark Lanzrein. Plain Porthault linen napkins and "Rat Tail" flatware fit with Constructivist simplicity into the black, red, white, and silver color scheme. Crystal balls are held in a freely arranged grouping of cut-crystal candlesticks. They, like the "Honeycomb" crystal stemware, catch and scatter a shimmer of candlelight about the subtly brilliant setting, which is completed by twentieth-century classic chairs and a plain white Portuguese carpet.

# FOOD
# FOR THOUGHT
## *Robert Currie and*
## *Christine Maly*

Any and all surrealistic or metaphysical conjecture is welcomed at this cantilevered black marble table designed by New York's "visual planners" and masters of fantasy Robert Currie and Christine Maly.

A gilded fish skeleton lies on a twenty-pound silver ingot rolled and polished by Tiffany's silver factory for this special occasion. Sterling silver shoehorns will serve gold-painted ostrich eggs from the fluid form of a modernist crystal bowl. A Peretti gold mesh pouch hangs in a crystal vase, and a black jade Peretti paper knife will deal with the black and gilt pebbles in a massive crystal ashtray. A seedpod box designed for Tiffany's by sculptor Charles Perry is lined in vermeil. The floral decoration is eighteen-karat gold, a tiger lily by Tiffany's Angela Cummings. A horse's skull surveying the scene sees that all glitters.

# DINNER FOR FOUR
## *Angelo Donghia*

From the man who invented the gray-flannel sofa and baptized his fabric and home furnishings house Vice Versa, design can legitimately expect a relaxed and freewheeling vision of formal dining.

In yet another unpredicted move, Angelo Donghia, that vaunt-courier of public taste, vaults his parchment-covered dinner table for four across an expansive sofa bed (both of his own design) and creates a setting to be examined attentively for the secrets of its uncommon elegance.

The bold patterns and robust forms of Tiffany's Mark Lanzrein's inlaid potteries act as foils for a strutting row of silver jiggers lined up and filled with a carefully edited selection of flowers, whose extreme formality repeats in an "Ovalis" vase where sand holds the most studied of leaf and flower arrangements.

A silver can pitcher holds wine; crystal spirals hold candles. Dinner silver is "Hampton," and the bamboo shaft propped against the bed is echoed by "Bamboo" fruit knives.

The bamboo, the raw silk upholstery, the Chinese Ming chairs, the dhurrie rug, and the aestheticism of floral design all speak of Angelo Donghia's fondness for oriental inspiration.

# DINNER
## *Douglas Fairbanks, Jr.*

A rhino plays the triangle, there's an elephant on the bass, and a buffalo crashes the cymbals at this Palm Beach dinner. Such antic behavior will, of course, be taken in stride by the host, Douglas Fairbanks, Jr., that knight errant of filmland who has made himself at home in roles from Rupert of Hentzau in *The Prisoner of Zenda* to Sinbad the Sailor.

No one would agree that "It's Tough to Be Famous" at this handsome table set with inlaid and painted earthenwares around a centerpiece of woven silver baskets planted with spring flowers.

The inlaid "Marble" pattern plates coordinate with candlesticks whose sinuous design comes from a fifteenth-century Ukrainian chintz. The silver is Tiffany's "Hampton." There are small earthenware baskets used as nut dishes, wine in simple carafes, and "St. Rémy" stemware.

There are white cotton upholstered Louis XV provincial chairs, and the animal musicians are by the Fairbankses' friend Spadini.

# COUNTRY SUPPER
# ON THE BACK PORCH
## *Mrs. Angier Biddle Duke*

The rigorously formal etiquette of embassy dinners that Mrs. Duke well knows from her years in the international diplomatic community stands aside here for a relaxed dinner on the Southampton summer house back porch.

For country tables, Mrs. Duke has always enjoyed making her own brightly patterned cloths, which retain a traditional and simple country theme while introducing dramatic interplays of color.

The intense contrasts of burnt orange with the cobalt and cornflower blues of the glazed chintz are repeated by the chrysanthemums and cornflowers massed in the unusually shaped wicker basket centerpiece. Blue napkins and the rich cobalts of "Blue Canton" reinforce the color statement.

Mrs. Duke chose boldly scaled "Metternich" paneled crystal goblets and wooden-handled silver wine caddies. They, like the classic "King William" flatware with its pistol-handled knives, are in perfect harmony with the eighteenth-century Chinese export ware–inspired "Blue Canton" china.

Small informal white ceramic baskets serve as salts and peppers. Crystal hurricane lamps protect candles from the evening breezes.

Polished oak French country dining chairs and straightforward gray-painted decking complete the setting's warm mixture of traditional country charm and the animating drama of a thoroughly contemporary color sense.

# HEART
# TO HEART
## *Mrs. Donald Newhouse*

Everything pink and white and strewn with hearts and flowers and tied in silver ribbons; crystal flutes of pink champagne and candles burning under a canopy of spring lilies and tulips—in short, a party as it surely ought to be with its atmosphere of charming unreality and its many engaging frivolities that disarm, seduce, and delight.

In this Valentine's Day dinner for four, Mrs. Donald Newhouse combines "Framboise Rose" and "Rose Plaid" Private Stock porcelain with "Chrysanthemum" flat silver. There are fresh violets for the ladies and candied violets for everyone, held in an antique pierced-silver heart dish. Pink napkins are tied with Tiffany designer Elsa Peretti's silver-mesh necklaces, and a variety of porcelain and silver heart boxes offer old-fashioned candies to mix with the old-fashioned sentiments of the evening.

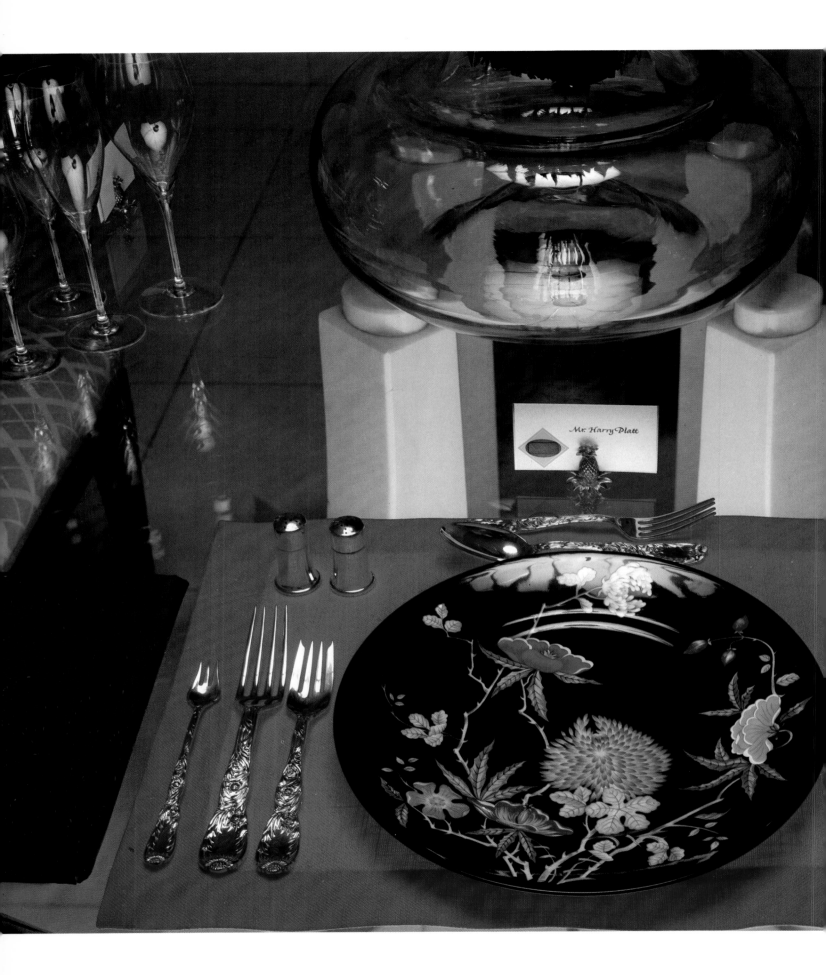

Mr. Harry Platt

# EXPOSURE
## *Mrs. John Murchison*

The spare lines and strong primary colors of Constructivism dominate this highly contemporary luncheon setting by Dallas hostess Lupi Murchison, whose witty excursions into the counterpoints of elaborately detailed "Chrysanthemum" flatware and "Famille Noir" enameled porcelain service plates only strengthen the carefully balanced modernism of the dining room's assertive interior.

A veritable geyser of pheasant feathers festively erupts from a crystal centerpiece. Oyster forks, bouillon spoons, and the four "Bruxelles" stemmed glasses at each place promise a festive, complex, and carefully structured meal.

# FORMALLY INFORMAL WINE CELLAR SUPPER

## *Mrs. James D. Robinson, Jr.*

---

The end of the nineteenth century produced a rich-textured eclecticism that combined Victorian and Napoleon III motifs with French, Japanese, and even Colonial Revival fashions. The South was particularly receptive to this all-embracing American "high style," and there it legitimately lives on in an air of tranquil security and well-being.

Mrs. James Robinson, Jr., of Atlanta sets her high-style wine cellar table with a central runner, placemats, and napkins of elaborate antique point de Venise lace. Golden cherubs decked in grapevines cavort about the base of a nineteenth-century French bronze-doré fruit stand. Heavily cut Irish "Ashford" stemware glitters in the candlelight, and Tiffany's "Hamilton" vermeil flatware gilds the setting with a somewhat delinquent echo of colonial America. The center of attention, however, is the stylish "Bigouden" Tiffany Private Stock hand-painted porcelain with its riveting yellow and blue Japanese Revival pattern.

# AT HOME ON THE AVENUE
## *Mrs. Seymour Berkson*

With the same composed assurance that guides her through the hazardous terrains of style and fashion in her public role as Eleanor Lambert, nationally syndicated columnist, originator of the Coty American Fashion Critics' Award, and impresario of the International "Best-Dressed List" poll, Mrs. Seymour Berkson receives eighteen for dinner in her Fifth Avenue apartment.

There is a mixture of festivity, simplicity, easy elegance, and abundance to the evening; and just as there is a relaxed eclecticism to the engaging collection of oriental and European ceramics that ornaments the dining room, there is a correspondingly informal mixture of compatible patterns on the buffet tables. "No one," says Mrs. Berkson, "really needs to have eighteen of anything."

Her central table, from which guests serve themselves fish and meat as well as salad and cheese, mixes "Rat Tail" and "King William" flat silver and two sizes of "Celadon" porcelain plates. The dessert table, watched over by a pair of covered vases in "Niello" pattern faience, includes three patterns of dessert plates: "Jardin de Jade" Private Stock, "Japanese Peony," and "Hokusai."

An extraordinary and early Ch'ien Lung blue and white Chinese porcelain screen dated 1745 and bought in Hong Kong by Mrs. Berkson dominates the candlelit room, which includes in its end niches a remarkable collection of "Red Anchor" Chelsea botanical plates.

# TEA AND COFFEE

---

Fin d'Été / Paloma Picasso

Le Café au Salon Rouge / Mme Émile Aillaud

Tea on the Porch / Suzanne and Carleton Varney

Tea for More Than Two / Mrs. John Pierrepont

Victoriana / Robert Denning and Vincent Fourcade

Sunday Tea / Mrs. Denton A. Cooley

The Fledermaus Café / after Josef Hoffmann: Tiffany & Co.

Dessert Party After the Winter Antiques Show Opening /
Mrs. Cruger D. G. Fowler

---

# FIN D'ÉTÉ
## *Paloma Picasso*

---

"I am a genius; my children are geniuses. They can take care of themselves," Picasso once explained to his youngest daughter during one of Paloma's not infrequent demands for his attention. It is still early in her career as theatrical set and costume and jewelry designer to tell to what extent this prophecy of that protean talent of twentieth-century art will be accurate; but in every detail of his daughter's designs there is evidence of a fresh, whimsical, and advanced imagination with a very personal flair for the original.

Picasso couldn't cook; and in this as in many ways, Paloma is her father's daughter. "I like to try things in the kitchen," she explains. "Sometimes I spend hours—and then we all go out for dinner."

Very much aware of the need for fantasy in our post–Lewis Carroll world, Paloma enjoys inviting friends to tea parties as delightfully outlandish as the Mad Hatter's.

Here she places her setting in the long-shadowed, surrealistic light of a September afternoon. Tall imaginary windows cast their elongated grid of painted sunlight on the floor.

The table groans with cakes and candies. "It's a dream tea party," Paloma says, "and I apparently have lots of sweet dreams."

The folding "party chair" covers, the tablecloth, and the napkins are all of white Eaglesham linen tied and festooned with silver bows and ribbons that repeat the motifs of Tiffany Private Stock "Green Cardinale" bone china. The "Chrysanthemum" flatware, the elaborately chased silver cookie jar, the gadrooned plates, and the swirled fluting of the silver tea set all contribute to the baroque look Paloma wanted for her table.

The March Hare is naturally present in the form of a silver rabbit-head beaker, and one of the Queen of Hearts' hedgehogs was going to act as a cake until Paloma decided his form wasn't exciting and had the pastry chef of the Four Seasons transform him into a mushroom. Red heart-shaped anthurium float above the table, which, besides its marzipan candies, frosted brioche cake, and *gâteaux secs* includes a pot of Bar-le-Duc red currant jam next to a silver cabbage filled with green mint jelly and a lavishly faceted crystal compote piled high with glistening French *fruits glacés,* which caught Paloma's temptable eye in a window of the Côte d'Azur.

# LE CAFÉ AU SALON ROUGE
## *Mme Émile Aillaud*

---

The "Red Room" of Paris hostess Charlotte Aillaud's St.-Germain-des-Prés house is one of those privileged spots informed by taste and sensibility where all is calm, luxurious, secure, voluptuous.

After luncheons in the Aillauds' Empire dining room, guests pause in this intimate salon before rejoining the outside life of 1980s France.

An oversized lacquer coffee table is the center of action. It holds an eighteenth-century French silver coffee service with "Fruit and Flowers" porcelain cups along with orchids, art books, silver "Heart Beakers" filled with pencils and violets, and a "Cerbère" crystal cube vase designed by Tiffany's Van Day Truex.

Sunlight from the garden filters in through painted silk muslin curtains.

A portrait of Mme Aillaud by Douglas Johnson sits below a fifth-century B.C. Greek torso. There is a drawing of the master of the house, the French urbanist/ architect Émile Aillaud, in the illuminated bookcase.

# TEA
# ON THE PORCH

## *Suzanne and Carleton Varney*

The easel holds a preliminary fabric design study signed "Carleton Varney." The white Wicker Garden furniture is cushioned in Carleton V's "Growing Wilder," whose tulips are repeated on a hand-painted pillow.

In the midst of directing the renowned design firm of Dorothy Draper, writing his nationally syndicated "Your Family Decorator" column, and producing the fabric lines of Carleton V, Carleton and Suzanne Varney take time out with their children for an old-fashioned summer tea party on the screened porch.

Traditional French country "Trianon" earthenware with its "Strasbourg tulip" coordinates with the fabrics. Its contours are echoed by Tiffany's "Flemish" sterling silver flatware. Lace napkins and Boston ferns carry on the Edwardian note of the white wicker.

A ceramic garden hat by George Sacco sits on the settee. The tea party cakes will be devoured by the Varneys' two young sons, Nicholas and Sebastian.

# TEA FOR MORE THAN TWO

*Mrs. John Pierrepont*

The Pierreponts' living room, looking out across the lyric New England landscape of their Far Hills estate, is the setting of daily afternoon teas. "Most of the time we're two," says Nancy Pierrepont, "but it might creep up to eight."

The tea tray includes an antique silver hot water kettle and a "Palmette" bone china tea service; antique silver caddies hold teas. There is a fresh home-baked cake and "Bamboo" flat silver, which was designed for Tiffany's by Van Day Truex, a long-time friend of the Pierreponts. (The ink wash drawing of an Italian church that hangs in the living room below a Walter Stumpfeig landscape is also by Truex.)

Flowers are from the Pierreponts' gardens and the household pets, Pounce and Arabella, look on. "Arabella," Mrs. Pierrepont explains, "was named for the former employer of our nanny and Pounce is just a name—like to pounce on a mouse."

# VICTORIANA
## Robert Denning and Vincent Fourcade

Napoleon's nephew Louis Napoleon Bonaparte ruled France for twenty-two years, first as President, then as the Emperor Napoleon III. The decorative styles of his 1852–1870 reign, like those of his British contemporary, Queen Victoria, were as deliciously complex and interlaid with cream filling as the celebrated puff pastry that bears his name.

The New York firm of Robert Denning and Vincent Fourcade, Inc., is America's unquestioned champion of Napoleon III–Victorian styles and excels at re-creating lively and extravagant period settings such as this Paris banker's salon of circa 1870.

A mahogany cellarette is placed before a trompe l'oeil window composed of a nineteenth-century Chinese panel painting whose summer palace garden is framed by lavish Napoleon III Aubusson tapestry portieres complete with deep valance and gold lace inner blind. The cellarette holds a dessert service of "Framboise Rose" Tiffany Private Stock porcelain, "Castilian" dessert forks, and pistol-handled knives. A pierced openwork tureen is flanked by a collection of other elaborately crafted sterling silver objects. On the cellarette shelf, wine in ring-necked decanters will be poured into glasses chilling in a silver Monteith bowl.

A "French Bronze" languidly surveys this credible picture of life in nineteenth-century Paris furnished with its green-tufted, leather-upholstered Napoleon III armchairs and settee, its tea table well stocked with "Framboise Rose," and its mid-nineteenth-century Bessarabian flowered rug.

# SUNDAY TEA
## *Mrs. Denton A. Cooley*

In the active Houston lives of the Cooleys, dinners for twenty-four are classified as "small" and guest lists not infrequently swell to such proportions that cocktail buffets become more practicable than seated dinners. Notwithstanding their delight in society, the Cooleys have a special fondness for their few private moments, which include Sunday afternoon teas alone.

"I like lots of flowers and a very romantic room," explains Mrs. Cooley.

Here in their "Portrait Room," designed by Houston architect John Staub, high tea awaits with its prolific array of cakes and fruits, its prettily embroidered napkins, and its romantically red tea roses from the Cooleys' garden. A superbly ornamented Adam Revival table and settee painted in the manner of Swiss/English neoclassicist Angelica Kauffmann and collected by Dr. Cooley furnish the setting and demand ornamented tablewares.

Mrs. Cooley answered the call with "Flora Danica" cups and saucers to match her "Flora Danica" fruit plates with their intricately pierced and gilded borders.

The flat silver is "English King." The silver tea set is of eighteenth-century French inspiration. Crystal fruit dishes offer clove-picked lemon slices, strawberries, and the delicate green interior traceries of halved kiwis.

Mrs. Cooley has made certain in this setting filled with subtle light and color and charm that no sense will be left stranded.

# THE FLEDERMAUS CAFÉ
## *after Josef Hoffmann: Tiffany & Co.*

In late 1907 the Café Fledermaus, designed, decorated, and outfitted by Josef Hoffmann, Kolomon Moser, and other members of the Wiener Werkstätte including Oskar Kokoschka and Gustav Klimt, opened at number 32 of Vienna's Kärntnerstrasse. This Secessionist art masterpiece immediately became the hub of Vienna's art world. Its black and white "checkerboard" tiled bar hummed with talk of art, architecture, music, drama, and politics mixed with rumors of both café society and the Hapsburg court of Franz Josef.

Tiffany's recaptures the spirit of the Fledermaus in this interior furnished with a set of original Josef Hoffmann Fledermaus furniture on the inevitable Hoffmann checkerboard floor. Coffee and Viennese cakes are served on "Black Bamboo" china. The silver is Tiffany "Bamboo." The water tumblers and pitcher are from designs by Secessionist architect Adolf Loos.

# DESSERT PARTY AFTER THE WINTER ANTIQUES SHOW OPENING

## *Mrs. Cruger D. G. Fowler*

Mrs. Cruger D. G. Fowler, 1980 co-chairman of New York's prestigious Winter Antiques Show, uses a selection from her remarkable collection of antique Tiffany silver in this setting for a dessert party.

Her flat silver is "Antique," a rare Tiffany engraved pattern custom-designed in the 1890s. Her sideboard holds, besides a modern Tiffany coffee service, covered tureen, and candlesticks, a repoussé chased pitcher richly ornamented with Chinoiserie patterns. The pitcher, marked "Tiffany, Young & Ellis" and made around 1850, is an extraordinary and important example of mid-nineteenth-century American silver.

Charles Louis Tiffany first went into the silver business after the store he founded in 1837 moved to 271 Broadway in 1847. He hired as his silver designer Gustav Herter, who was to become one of the most celebrated designer/decorators of his day. From Herter's penchant for oriental motifs it can legitimately be suspected that this pitcher is of his design.

To compliment her antique family silver, Mrs. Fowler chooses Royal Worcester hand-painted "Imari" dessert plates, "Hong Kong" demitasse cups, and intricately cut "Gabriel" crystal.

Tablecloths are "Vanessa" print from Clarence House. Repoussé chased beaker centerpieces are from Tiffany's modern silver collections. The ladies' silver-mesh and woven-bamboo evening bags are by Tiffany designer Elsa Peretti; and "The Rose of Sharon," a romantic nineteenth-century portrait by Shephard Alonzo Mount, watches over the proceedings.

# THE GREAT OUTDOORS

The Golfer's Lunch / Bob Hope
"Roughing It" with a Picnic / Mrs. Alfred Kennedy
Eternal Triangle / Gene Moore
Veranda Picnic / Mrs. Henry Parish II
The Mysterious, Romantic Picnic on the Shores of
Lake Michigan / Suzanne Clarke Falk
Dinner at the Beach / Tiffany & Co.
Hunting Picnic / Diana Rigg

# THE GOLFER'S LUNCH
## *Bob Hope*

Bob Hope once said that he was on the road so much that his wife, Dolores, had the towels in their bath marked "Hers" and "Welcome Traveler." When the grand master of the topical wisecrack and universally loved veteran of countless films, radio programs, TV shows, and personal appearances was not delighting audiences with his "songs, patter, and eccentric dancing," he was probably playing golf.

Here on the terrace that overlooks the private fairway of his new Palm Springs house, he takes time off for lunch after a morning's sport.

The simple wicker and glass table is set with "Carnation" earthenware plates and Tiffany's "Hampton" flat silver. There are crystal "Bamboo" mugs for iced tea from an Adolf Loos–designed crystal pitcher. A trompe l'oeil pottery cabbage holds citrus fruits.

The Hopes' terrace takes full advantage of the Southern California mountains' panoramic beauty.

# "ROUGHING IT" WITH A PICNIC
## *Mrs. Alfred Kennedy*

---

The Kennedys' twelve-room Palladian villa sits above the Chattahoochee River on a hill in Atlanta. The elaborate marble detailing of its neo-Mannerist façade by architect James Means offers a delightful backdrop for one of the informal terrace "picnic" meals the outdoors-loving Kennedys enjoy.

"We used to entertain on a much grander scale when Alfred was president of the Opera Association," recalls Virginia Kennedy. "Now we relax and have more informal groups."

The Kennedys' love of gardening is reflected by the floral motifs of French "Panier Chinois" porcelain, whose patterns are repeated on hand-embroidered table linen. A pure crystal globe vase designed by Tiffany's Van Day Truex for Baccarat catches the reflection of the Palladian façade. "Shell and Thread" flat silver and "St. Rémy" crystal stemware retain the note of neoclassicism so inextricably linked with the comforts of southern living.

# ETERNAL TRIANGLE

## *Gene Moore*

By his arresting and unexpected juxtaposi-tioning of not obviously compatible elements, Gene Moore has been dazzling strollers on Fifth Avenue since 1955 with his Tiffany window displays.

"Display is," Mr. Moore has said, "an art of night"; and here, at this dinner for three set in a forest clearing, darkness again sets off his magical handiwork.

Nature provided the flowered cloth of moss from the forest floor with lilies of the valley sprouting here and there.

Tiffany's provided the man-made flowers of "Navarre" porcelain and "Chrysanthemum" vermeil flatware.

Sociable butterflies inspect the flower arrangement while lobs and goblins wait in the woods to catch a glimpse of the arriving trio.

# VERANDA PICNIC
## *Mrs. Henry Parish II*

For generations the name "Sister Parish" has been magic in the design world. The exuberant wealth of ideas Mrs. Parish brings to every job, the vitality and charm of her interiors, the abundance of her design vocabulary have made her a legend.

In this spring picnic buffet conjured up with her habitual flair, she charms her audience with the illusions of a rich collection of trompe l'oeil potteries. The eggs and vegetables, the artichokes, asparagus, cabbage, melon, carrots, squash, and radishes are pure illusion. The eye is tricked—and at once delighted.

Under the striped awning, there will be real drinks in "Earth" mugs, and there is food enough for the eye not only in Sister Parish's assemblage of Tiffany trompe l'oeil but in the country flowers, the wicker furnishings, and the amusing needlepoint pillows.

# THE MYSTERIOUS, ROMANTIC PICNIC ON THE SHORES OF LAKE MICHIGAN

## *Suzanne Clarke Falk*

In the late 1800s, "beach cottage" meant something solidly constructed of cut stone with upwards of twenty-eight rooms and preferably situated on Newport's Bellevue Avenue. Our more modest late-1900s counterpart in upper-crust understatement is surely the "beach picnic," which easily demands more elaborate preparation than Trimalchio's feasts. Beach towels, army blankets, paper plates, thermos bottles, potato salad, and deviled eggs emerging from worn wicker hampers have been supplanted by oriental flatweave carpets, silver and lots of it, fine ceramics, decorative accessories, and international specialty foods washed down with *les grands crus de France.*

Here young Chicago socialite Suzanne Clarke Falk prepares to entertain guests at a lakeside picnic where the pervasive sense of unreality is strictly intentional.

Autumn mists roll in from Lake Michigan in the background. Snorkel equipment along with a serape have been jauntily abandoned by a beach chair screened from the clement elements by an embroidered Indian umbrella.

Lunch awaits on a fine Afghan cotton dhurrie rug in appropriate shades of sand, indigo, sun-bleached green, and brick. The insistent zigzags of the dhurrie's field are picked up by the abstract patterns of an assortment of Tiffany inlaid earthenware dishes in natural earth colors. There is ample silver, a stockpot to hold bread, an oriental footed dish for spareribs, Van Day Truex's "Seed Pod" tureen used as a wine cooler, "Bamboo" flatware, silver beakers holding a variety of accessory foods, and a pair of trout-head toasting cups.

The hostess again raises questions of reality in the equivocal and evanescent setting by mixing Este trompe l'oeil ceramics with the actual food. The nuts, scallions, and small dish of eggs are all painted pottery. The flowers by McAdams of Lake Forest, the driftwood, and the romantic mood are real.

# DINNER
# AT THE BEACH
## *Tiffany & Co.*

Champagne and sausages; the throwaway look of polished silver sitting in the sand; the jumbled boundaries between sophistication and simplicity; the absolute attraction of opposites: in sum, the mannered elegance of formal beach picnics presents itself in all its subtleties to the knowing eye with this summer fête.

Each diner enjoys an individual wicker tray set with one of Tiffany's oversize, inlaid earthenware "Fish" plates, sterling salt and pepper, crystal tumbler, "Bamboo" sterling flat silver, and blue and white mattress-ticking napkins. The cylinders for condiments, the champagne cooler, and fruit bowl are all fine stoneware.

A profusion of baskets, trays, fans, and fish traps of wicker and bamboo structure the setting, and their primitive qualities enhance the superb craftsmanship of the silver and stonewares.

# HUNTING PICNIC
## *Diana Rigg*

Life with that one-man orchestra of espionage and global troubleshooting James Bond was no picnic in Connecticut, as Diana Rigg, the lovely leading lady of British thrillers, so beautifully demonstrated "on Her Majesty's Secret Service." Yet the lady had experience, and after years of starring in "The Avengers" it was a well-practiced hand that Miss Rigg brought to the fast and perilously glamorous world of Ian Fleming's Agent 007; and it is that same practiced hand she brings here to staging a hunt picnic in pure luxury-promoting James Bondian style.

Rolls-Royce Motors, Ltd., has seen to it that Miss Rigg and her entourage hunt in proper comfort and that the "boot" of her Standard Silver Shadow will be spacious enough to hold a silver Tiffany punch bowl filled with ice, Dom Pérignon, and chilled champagne flutes, as well as a butler's table from Florian Papp (to hold her silver Tiffany tea service) and all the many baskets of rare and tempting delicacies prepared by the chefs of New York's Soho Charcuterie in CinemaScopic proportion. Her properly prodigal country feast includes pheasant, rabbit, and duck terrines laced with fruits and nuts. The fresh fruits and vegetable salads are naturally both